Apostle of Desire

Apostle of Desire

Poems

Bruce Weigl

AMERICAN POETS CONTINUUM SERIES NO. 214

BOA EDITIONS, LTD. * ROCHESTER, NY * 2025

Manufactured in the United States of America

First Edition
23 24 25 26 7 6 5 4 3 2 1

Publications by BOA Editions, Ltd.—a not-for-profit corporation under section 501 (c) (3) of the United States Internal Revenue Code—are made possible with funds from a variety of sources, including public funds from the Literature Program of the National Endowment for the Arts; the New York State Council on the Arts, a state agency; and the County of Monroe, NY. Private funding sources include the Max and Marian Farash Charitable Foundation; the Mary S. Mulligan Charitable Trust; the Rochester Area Community Foundation; the Ames Amzalak Memorial Trust in memory of Henry Ames, Semon Amzalak, and Dan Amzalak; and contributions from many individuals nationwide. See Colophon on page 115 for special individual acknowledgments.

Cover art and Design: Sandy Knight
Interior Design and Composition: Isabella Madeira
BOA Logo: Mirko

BOA Editions books are available electronically through BookShare, an online distributor offering Large-Print, Braille, Multimedia Audio Book, and Dyslexic formats, as well as through e-readers that feature text to speech capabilities.

Cataloging-in-Publication Data is available from the Library of Congress.

BOA Editions, Ltd.
250 North Goodman Street, Suite 306
Rochester, NY 14607
www.boaeditions.org
A. Poulin, Jr., Founder (1938-1996)

Contents

hoang vắng

những ngọn đồi
mọc ra vừa đủ
Cho loài người
đổ bóng qua tôi

abandoned

these hills
rise enough
for humanity
they shade over me the abandoned

—Trần Lê Khánh, tr. BW

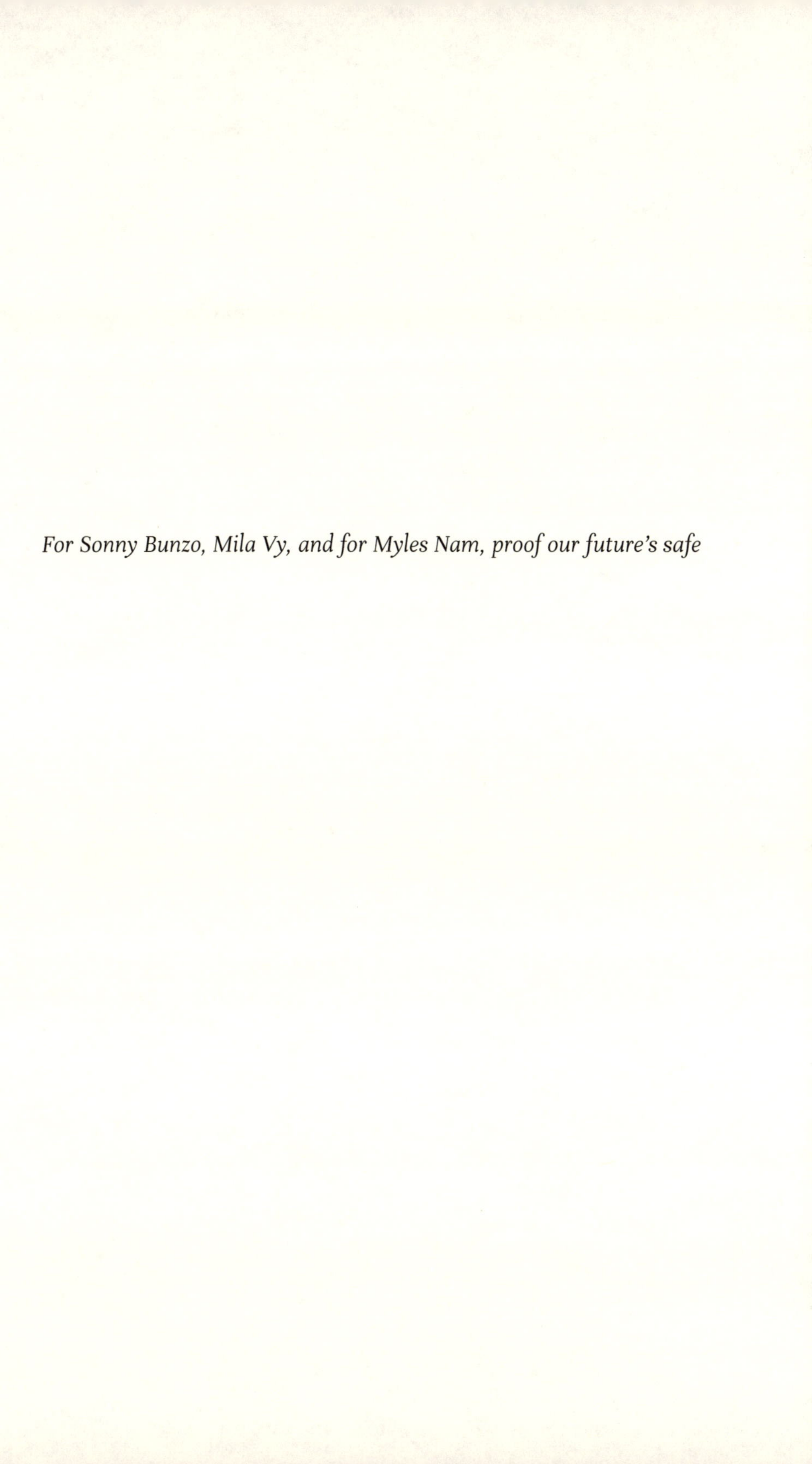

For Sonny Bunzo, Mila Vy, and for Myles Nam, proof our future's safe

To the Reader

If you bought my book and you're reading this
          and you don't like what you see
                    and you want your money back,
          I'm happy to oblige.

I've been in the same situation
          more than a few times in my life
                    I can tell you that.
          All it took was a few bad poems

and I wanted out.
          I wanted my hard-earned money
                    back, or at least a trade option
          for something more lyrically compelling.

I want you to feel free to do the same,
          although it's not like I have a portfolio
                    of alternative metaphors
          that I can substitute on a moment's notice

for the ones you find troubling,
          although perhaps I should,
                    nothing like
          the Well Rope Star of Barbarians

to keep your interest.
          Stay with me.
                    You worked so hard to get here,
          no point in leaving now.

My Corona Landslide

I'm inside of a mind
where the river's been blown out
wall of blood cascading
just behind me so I run
fast even after
everything that's happened. I stay ahead
of the wall of blood. I stay ahead.
I know not to ask
questions about the origin of pain
or about the screams that tear
the flawless sky to shreds
right before our eyes.
I know that much. A thing
that hunts us all keeps us
apart, it wants to kill
as many as it can. You'll walk
along the lake tonight without
my hand around your hand,
your voice inside my heart,
you'll walk alone for this
is how it is and I
won't pray for any god
to save us from ourselves

but I will hold the whole of you
inside of me,
the blood a darkened purple
wave, not here, not far away.

Loving the Jungle Blues

I'm out alone to have my private thoughts,
        how I must keep my heart
out in the dark,
        so I can be the jungle's
green again. I want

to be inside the arms
        of ambush, but darkness holds me back,
won't let me fly past stars
        that light the way, and distance
is a wall that I can't climb,

        but I know blue sky from pain,
and although my body rests tonight,
        an ocean between us,
my true heart is too wild to contain,
        so it flies to you, a rooster

in the tree, a thousand swallows
        someone names before they fly away.
Oh holy breath, your jungle
        mouth against my mouth,
your lips my sweet persuasion.

Tender Lotus

I pass several gates where the withered
lotus of last year want to sink
their secrets to the bottom of the pond

but instead, they lift the bright
young leaves out of the water
as if showing off their young.

Take care my love. If we can't
meet in summer,
I'll send you all the lotus from the pond.

The Preponderance of the Great Splitting Apart, (Homage to Emily D.)

It's best to stay on the edge of things
    when you're dealing with most people.

Imagine you're on a riverbank,
    the flooded river only feet

away. You can see the largest rocks
    stick up through the water which always

finds a way around the rocks.
    From where you stand,

you can trace the river by following the current,
    but if you enter the water,

it would be impossible to see. You would
    struggle to hold onto a branch,

or to find a resting place
    on one of the rocks,

or you would splash your way
    back to shore.

Better to stay on the edge
    where you can see everything

and still
    breathe good air

instead of river water, the way it's best
to pay attention to your own

orbit because of how easy it is
to spin off into trouble.

I want you here with me. The problem
isn't time, but space.

I don't know if you ever
hacked through a forest of green bamboo

under fire, but it's a lot like that. It's not
the time it takes to do that, see,

or the time it takes to die,
or to watch someone else die,

but the space you have to conquer
with your body, and it's best to do this

from the edge of things, to try and stay
out of the muck, listening

more carefully to everything. I want to rivet my own hands
together in prayer,

and find the single tone
that carries me to empty.

Don't laugh. No, I'm wrong,
go ahead, laugh.

Mưa Xuân

Spring rain is that finest mist you feel
        fall across your face like lace,
no room for your umbrella
        to pass on the crowded street,

so I keep it closed, my shirt
        already soaking through,
beads of sweat small pearls
        down my face. *Mưa Xuân*,

my friend says,
        as we make our way down
busy spring rain streets,
        and the murder of sensuous detail

is not a metaphor,
        you have to feel the waves of history
vibrate through you
        before you know anything at all.

Written the Day X. Left Prison

(One who keeps tearing apart his or her own wounds.

"The vertiginous knowledge that nothing is what there is,
and first of all, nothing beyond."

When yourself   with evidence   ends with wound).

Always, there was the terrible, and there was the beauty.
There was a hollowness in the chest,
and an insomnia of kisses,
so why do we demand

angels in the end to carry us off
and not the demons they resemble
is a question better not to raise among the minor officials,
but a lesson not too late for the learning,

like the reconsideration of the hornet's nest:
to smash or not to smash, that is the question.

Thinking About Her

River
white trees
who remembers
the statue's sad face

Outside Quảng Trị City, 1968

I'm watching out the window the cat stalk
the robin pulling up worms don't say a
word so I must be complicit when
you fire into the dark trees when you
fire round after round into the dark trees
without knowing who hides there until we stop

All I Need is all I Need

The heavy snow has covered all the trees,
it fell at night while we were both asleep.
It came to us while we were in
our separate dreams, that carried us away

while wind howled songs that sounded like a dirge.
At three a.m. the silence woke me up
and something stirred inside my damaged brain,
a door that I know well was opened up

and in flew all the haunted memories.
The worst is being trapped inside a hole
we'd dug at night to hide when rockets came.
The sound just like a train, that whoosh, I swear,

that we can never stop from coming back.
A sulfur smell can set it off, a noise
too loud and unexpected, all it takes.
But this is not a plea to anyone

for help or love of any kind.
My testimony's written for the trees,
who gather all around me in their care,
their many bending branches, all I need.

Verse Thirteen

The lonely
just before dawn
watch out in the dark
a single white light
bob in the trees
as if it meant nothing

this is how
things slip through the wire

Evening Before Desire, Hà Nội

I hear through my open window
someone hammering in a practiced rhythm
with only small pauses between pieces
of siding going up nearby,
and someone else playing the flute,
whose heavy notes hang in the ivy, like sorrow.

Forgiveness is overrated, the teacher says,
just another construct to deal with,
as if hearts could be untangled from each other,
like the long wire that time is, and only your fate left twisting.

Even darkness cannot be relied upon,
and all that you can do is call out
to the world, the one song that you know,
as if someone may hear it, and call you back.

Victim of Love

An avalanche of grief
 rolls over you,
a landslide of despair,

and although the morning air
 is filled with bird song,
they do not sing for you,

nor do the flowers that fight to open
 pay you any mind,
marked as the fool

who lost his one great love,
 empty of the joy he'd felt
just to hear her say his name,

or to hear her laugh,
 like a song it felt,
and you'll wait for the night

sky to rise above, like the shadow
 of a shadow, so you can ask
your weary questions to the stars

that shined when you held each other's
 hearts in the thousand-year-old city,
but even night has given up,

and there is no next chance for you to wait for,
 no next day, and no next night,
and no next anything.

The First Time I Heard Your Name, it was Different

The gradual burst of new lotus on the pond
          opening like tiny minds to the wonder,

          your hand on my shoulder
all that I need of the free world

Autumn, End of Everything

Trees bare
of leaves,
they show their age and rattle
when the wind is up
to make a sound like bones
down dark hallways. How can I
say so you understand
the thing I feel most deeply?
You have so many languages,
how can I pretend
to tell you how suddenly
autumn
transports us all to winter, a gift,
and how can I feel,
even through the dark miles,
the warm
blood of you, against me?

Attending a Meeting of High Officials

To harbor wild thoughts I believe is a good thing
from time to time, and then to try and connect them
all the way back to the world. To force us to love
god, as children, they made us be afraid with the catechism,
so that even the shadows, well, you know what the shadows do.
Just be frank, just say: what do you want with me, spirits?

The Dangers of Searching the Photographs of Reynaldo Sandoval

I'd thought about death, watching her sleep that day,
although I knew it wasn't sleep that the dead
practice, but something like sleep. A rock
bridge collapses to make a chasm too wide
to cross safely. A man is holding another man's
head by reaching in through the bars of a cage
hung from the ornate ceiling by a chain. Somewhere
the sky at dusk is filled with birds. Somewhere
a woman's face is gullied by the rivers
of her years, her beauty
finding refuge in her dark eyes. If we were
generous by nature, there would be enough for everyone,
but we're not, and whose fucking plan was that I wonder?
I saw an elephant carved into the sheer face
of a cliff by ancient hands and I could only
weep. Deserts stretched out before me, my only
tender escape. Kissing, the man and the woman
melt into each other's faces. There were some
words of Lorca, some cities, drowned in their own light.

Sky

Green everywhere. Green grass, green leaves, green bushes, green, new plants
and such a stillness in the air as you have never seen,
not a single leaf of grass stirring, not even the smallest maple leaves
high in the trees
where the spirits hide until the sun goes down. Above us is only sky,
whose bottom layers are blue and streaked with gray and white,
not like a painting exactly, but more like a bottomless opening to wonder.
This is where I see you waiting for me. I see you standing on a city street corner,
the busy traffic buzzing, something like a halo of light, all around your face.

Epistolary to a Brother

I thought one thing, and you thought another.
I said one thing and you heard whatever you wanted
to hear, but isn't that how it goes sometimes,
and don't we each create our own world of meaning
around our selves then live inside it like a bubble.
I don't know if a friendship means a straight line,

or if sometimes the graph falls off the charts.
The teacher chided me for being so attached
to words that someone else had said,
or to words at all.
How can you possess what isn't there, he scoffed.
I know he's right. I know that I am weak
to let myself be hurt by someone else's acts,
but you have to understand
what it meant to me to get those words.
In my life, at the time, there was nothing.

How Odd Our Grief

I was drawn-out, stretched thin dead friends
floating all around me,
even a few dead from the war
still humping through my dreamless

nights. I don't know how long a thing
like that can last in your head,
maybe forever, which isn't
that long, it turns out,

and there's nothing
stunning about your own losses,
or about the pain you imagined
could only be yours. Isn't

the world like that, doesn't it
make you pay and pay
in all the ways that no one
else can know or understand?

The New Road Neighborhood Showdown

The B-flat sound of heavy equipment
backing up between orange barrels,
loud metal slammed into metal,
some long-time neighbors
gather along the curb, grumbling,
to watch the new road go in,

and although I stand nearby,
their gossip is a code that I can't break,
and I don't know why I'm always on the verge,
looking in as if through the windows of a house
where I'm no longer welcome,
all the family gathered happily at the long table.

Heavy rollers filled with water finish the job.
They shape a seamless black ribbon driving back and forth,
and then they're gone, the trucks move far enough
away so the back-up warning horn is faint
through morning air,
a tugboat calling through the Erie fog.

I like a life like this,
a little wonder, everywhere you look,
the great possibilities
open
like an unlit doorway,
the new road finished
all the way to hell.

Empty

When the words
want to come
they crawl into my body
like those fat green
worms who devour
tomato plants
overnight
and fill me up.

That's what it's like these days,
so gorged with words
I wonder how it feels
to finally have nothing to say.

A Simple Lesson

Resist being tangled in a sloppy void,
is how I translated
what the teacher said to me
over hot tea
that was waiting when I'd arrived,
unannounced,
at the temple on the mountain in Hue.
How could even the dusty paths
shine
where the teacher walked
in his long robe?
How could the trees seem so green
I could feel them
grow inside me?

He tried to teach me
how knowing
was not knowing
but my skills were weak
and I could only smile,
so he told me the story
of the monkey
who was chained
to a coconut tree
nearby
and who lived his life
on a small wooden platform
the teacher had built.
It was cruel to keep him chained that way
the teacher said,

but the monkey had become
destructive
and clever enough
to get into the locked food bins,
so the teacher had carried him
for three days and nights into the jungle,
and released him into his new world
and to the other wild monkeys
where he quickly disappeared.

But by the time the teacher
had made his way
back through the thick jungle
to the temple,
the monkey had already returned,
and was waiting for the teacher
to feed him. Resist
being tangled in a sloppy void.

Why I Love my Doctor

the way I love sweet Ohio peaches
come late summer
if they survive the killer frost
I've seen this happen
too many times,
but when she asks me
to tell her what it is
that I'm afraid of
I have to say
that I'm afraid of her
for asking me that question.

Not every fucking thing
is reducible to words,
and why should it be?
There are some things that words
don't want anything to do with,
although I feel most safe
inside of words. Some people
I would forgive
practically anything.
Others
don't stand a chance,
even with the mercy
that flows through me.

Here I am

Now it all makes sense,
the bed wetting,
the belt beatings from my father,
the murderous misunderstandings
that led to a river of pain for everyone,
my enormous struggles in school,
and my too many questions.
I have always known that something was wrong,
something was off,
a gyro tilted too far to one side
so that everything looks different to me,
but makes its own sense.
As a kid I wondered why no one would help me
understand the world
according to my own odd mapping of things,
but I gave up and I began to practice
the art of living two lives at once,
one in which I could convince
everyone that I knew what I was doing,
and the other in which I allowed myself
to be the happy, mad boy who loved most
his time alone in the woods with birds and singing trees.

But the war had designs on me,
and I had to let go the spirit creature
I had been through all those years
so I could be counted on
when rockets slammed in
and men who wanted us dead
tangled in the wire, not far away.

I don't remember all the details, so don't press me.
I don't remember how we survived,
given my distinctive place,
but here I am.

My Bill Evans

I hear the wren's call
come in through the window
over the jazzy piano
the man plays

with all the pain of the lonely
until the two sounds
overlap

I don't know why
it should be so difficult
to feel

Small Autumn Festival Song for Xia Lu

Over the phone she told me
the story of the crickets

and for that depth of feeling
I was not prepared

Autumn festival
waiting under an enormous yellow moon

Loving the Thái Bình River Ghosts

I know this Hồ Chí Minh City
rain
is no different than rain anywhere else
once you get right down to the rain-ness of things,
although it falls from the sky
across the south China Sea
in drops as large as rice bowls. I know

even this far from home there are ghosts,
but the dead all speak the same language. Speak to me in your language,
rattle your bones to make a beat
that carries us away.

The Quality of Mental Health Care at the VA

1

You may live long enough to outgrow any illnesses they won't treat because of your age.

"I'm sorry, sir, the VA has determined that you are too old to be saved from this illness. The best we can do is make you comfortable."

I would never ask to be comfortable. Something's wrong with that thinking. It's inhumane. Most folks would agree that we should always do what we can to make the lives of those around us, animal, and human, better, most significantly when it comes to how long a life can be. "VA policy says that because of your age, you no longer qualify for this surgery, even though you need it. Even though it could lengthen your life."

These are not actual recordings, but they're close enough, and no less valuable as evidence in the case against the state

for the crime of the abuse of walking corpses, in field jackets.

2

Top Secret Umbra: Treatment Program 1.

When they come for help, tell them to go away.

Tell them that science says there's nothing wrong with them.

Sustain the precise nature of this paradigm for exactly eleven years,

until two hundred suicides a day begin to occur.

3

Top Secret Umbra: Treatment Program 2.

Give them drugs to stop how they feel about anything except more drugs. Three-month prescriptions are encouraged. Take a handful of these and a scoopful of those. Dispense this treatment freely and without consideration of anything except dulling the spirits of wounded souls as if they had no story tell.

4

Top Secret Umbra 3: The Variety of Cognitive Treatment Protocols.
Agree with everything they say.
Never trap them in the corner.
Teach them to create alternative realities
that they imagine may sustain them.
The end of feeling is the truest death,
once you've been to see the elephant.

The Inevitability of Things

Small pencil-thin snake
    swimming against the strong current, trapped in time,
as if anything was possible

those Saigon nights
    when I ran free
with my weapon
    and swam against my own black-market currents.

Just eighteen, but my Vietnamese friends
    had taught me the spoils of war,
and overnight
    I went from rocket and mortar attacks in the field

to hanging out in the city
    with my taxi driver mama-san connection,
so don't waste your algorithms on me,
    my suffering prefers not to be quantified,
yet look how far the snake has swum.

Why I Flunked Philosophy 301

"If you didn't know that the dog lived next door,
did it still bark,"
was my answer to the final exam essay question,
the result of which put me clearly
at the bottom of the class.
I don't know why
I didn't get it.
I loved my wacky professors
who could go on for hours
about the nature of promising,
or about the relative meaning of being. My favorite
was a man who discouraged me
from any further philosophical pursuits,
but did it in the kindest way imaginable.
I loved to watch his mind unfold into lectures.
On the small wooden podium,
he lined up the filters of cigarettes
he'd smoked in class along the way. To me
they looked exactly like soldiers
standing in formation on the tarmac,
waiting to deploy.

Being and Listening

What the night bird doesn't know
can hurt her. Any bird
who lives in the dark
should be watched closely
for signs of any diminishment
of interest in the State
and in what the State says is the truth.

Night bird in the black sky,
what is love?
Can it be a simple promise between hearts,
the names of longing
written across the sheer face of cliffs
impossible to climb?

Waiting for my Father's Bus

After weeks in muggy Hồ Chí Minh City,
the Hà Nội air is cool in April,
the city greening towards spring. I don't know
if the ghosts who join me on the evening
streets are real, or imagined, but
I know it doesn't matter, a long
time since I'd lifted that veil to see
the absolute sameness of things. As a child
this confused and sometimes frightened me.
As a child on whom grownups had put
their greedy hands, I knew things. Sometimes,
the dead have shown themselves to me.
Growing up in that house of no books,
I was filled with words that seldom made
sense enough to interest the grownups around me.
I saw things as a child for which
there was no sensible explanation.
One autumn Ohio day I played
in the vacant lot next to our crumbling
apartment. Overgrown with weeds and wild
grass that no one cared to mow,
it was another world to me,
my private kingdom in which I did
my private things. Early afternoon
I was alone in the lot when the sky turned dark.
I wanted to call out to my mother or father,
but they were at work. The neighbors,
in whose sloppy care my sister and I
had been delivered by our too young parents,

sipped cheap wine all day from coffee
mugs, and seldom left the ratty
sofa where they sat together
watching black and white day-
time television, circa 1950 something.
They were there but of no use to me that day
in the lot next door, so I stayed quiet
and found refuge in the weeds
and brambles and watched the dark sky
get darker. I saw two girls, I thought,
walking casually down the street
in my direction, and I was happy
to see them and hoped they might know what
was going on with the sky. They wore
matching club jackets. They looked
like teenagers from a distance but as they got
closer, their whole countenance changed.
I saw a light I'd never seen
before, flood out from what looked like
open cracks in the skin of one of the girls.
The light was too bright, and I had to turn
away but when I moved, I attracted
their attention. One of them left the sidewalk
and walked towards me where I'd imagined
I lay hidden in the weeds. The sky was black.
The trees were empty of birds. No traffic
passed, and the quiet frightened me.
As a child I imagined that death and life
were the same, only a slim door
between the two ways of being.
I wasn't afraid of dying. Already

I knew there were things worse than death.
But I was afraid of getting lost
in a way of being that felt like
it was descending all around me,
a sticky net. I was lonely. I knew
that word to the bone and I allowed myself
to leave it on my lips to linger
like a kiss. A hum that grew louder
and that I could feel push the skin
against my bones filled the empty lot.
I watched images of what had been
our poor life click past like slides
in a projector. Some of the images were comforting,
but others forced me to remember
the belt and the not having,
and the hands that didn't belong.
"Don't worry," one of the girls said, "you'll be okay."
She was carrying a sign covered with symbols
I couldn't make sense of although I can draw them
even today. The other girl carried
two buckets that I understood
were filled with blood. "For the others," she said. My body
trembled like I was cold. I couldn't
move until the light began
to fill the sky again, and the teenage
girls were gone on their ragged wings.
The starlings had returned to the trees
where they chattered like gossipy neighbors. Later
that afternoon
I sat on the stoop of Bonk's bar and waited
for the bus to bring my father

home from work. I had some things to say
to him. I hoped that I could
find the words to let it all make sense.
I hoped that he would listen.

Bodies

Is it only bodies
not desperately tangling together for once
in a rented room
in the thousand-year-old city,

or is there more than that?
We own only what we can give away
and we believe that includes even our hearts.
Later, in the Blue Bird Nest Café on Đặng Dung street,

the two lives had already begun to pull apart,
the only solution when the script fails
and longing is allowed to blossom
like lotus,

all across the pond's dark face.
There's no light today, but that of sacrifice,
yet how much room there is for sacrifice
among the wounded, in the small café.

Tôi đi bộ quanh hồ Hà Lê

The practical rules over everything here,
where I like to spend my time
walking around lake Hà Lê
after lunch, the sun

bright on the water and fishermen
either cast a line with meaty bait
or use a treble hook
to snag. Not the best time

to try and catch fish,
I know—

from my own fishing Lake Erie
where I grew up among
the working poor, and caught fish

to help feed our family,
and later in the gorgeous limestone
creeks of central Pennsylvania
where I stalked brown trout with a fly rod

that the fish like to stay out
of the sun during the hottest part of the day.
They find their way to the shade
of a willow tree on the ragged shore,
just off the pull of current
and moving river. They won't move
much, not even to feed,
or do anything, except drift just off the flow

of water, as it moves
away. I watch the fishermen
pull in fish after fish
from the still lake, and let them die

on the concrete bank. I ask
the man how he's catching so many
fish in the sun, in the middle
of the day, and he tells me that his family is hungry.

The Weight of Rain

I return to become a wanderer.
I borrow her lipstick's stain
of love affairs which float and drown

onto this shore
before the thousand flower petals
and the storm
fills the dust.

The Ambiguity of His Intentions

I waited in a bar in Cambridge for my teacher
while he did some poetry business at Harvard, lucky
graduate student I was after the war
who had found someone who took interest
in my poor work and in the man I hadn't yet
become. I was killing time and thought I might
drink my way through the long afternoon.
Later, I would be driven home by my teacher,
and I had no other chores.
I was drinking Irish Whiskey and cold
draft beer, slowly, as I watched a baseball game
in black and white that had gotten suspended in time
by the rain. I sat alone among others. We shared
a little baseball over drinks, but no one
said too much or even said their names.
A black and white cat walked across the room.
The door swung open. Someone else had come
to drink. He sat two stools down from me
and that was fine. I feel better when people
don't get too close. He joined us to watch the game
and threw down two vodka shots before
he took his hat off. He chased the shots with a bottled
beer and tapped the bar with his empty shot glass
for another. We were on our way. What did I know
about anything. He bought my drinks throughout the afternoon.
The barflies came and went. He asked me questions
about the war. Someone played an accordion
in a back room. I didn't know how drunk I was
until I tried to stand up to find the head and fell
directly onto the floor with my face. My new

friend helped me up, nameless, he wiped
the blood away with his handkerchief, and gave me
another drink. He moved to the bar stool next to mine
and he put his hand on my leg. He asked me if I'd been wounded
in the war. I told him it was none of his business,
but because he wasn't done with me
he asked if he could see the place where the wound had healed.

Apostle of Desire

The brightest green parrot
squawks from the marbled-floor living room
where no one lives,

style over function
lost on me and

whatever seductions
went way over my head
at the dinner party

busy with servants.

All morning long it had rained
so hard even the toad

took refuge in my room,
the purple sky.

Lost Episode

Rain settles in like a pack of
guests
just back
from the dusty road

and more rain on the way, drops
big as rice bowls
swept across the south China sea, why

promises must be kept
to the empty,

Homage to the Gecko

Grateful for the swift work she
makes of mosquitoes and flies
I wait for her to come out
from behind things
where she fits her slim body
to stay cool I imagine
until the sun goes down

she is thin as an envelope
she is brown going to green
and we have chosen
to live here together

our dark rooms
more than enough
for the two of us
to hide from everything
except the dust of worlds
crumbling far away in space
that find you in the end.

Saying Goodbye to Achill

At a certain age
goodbye begins to mean
something.
One fine poet friend
warned me against writing about the sheep,
and although I understood what he meant,
I also knew that the black-faced
scraggly ewes
with their lambs in the grassy bogs
would find their way into my dreams,
and what else could I do
but let them have their way
one cold windy Cabaun day
when they'd stood in a circle
around a single fallen sister,
the gimp we'd watched get worse
finally taking her down.
Determined to keep out
whatever tried to get in,
they stayed that way all morning.
I had business at the pub.
I left her lying there, soundlessly
among her brethren,
and when I returned,
part of the landscape
had fallen off into the sea.

A Vision

The garden's drunk with flowers
not waiting for anything
except what they had coming.
My love, I thought I had coming,
shadow of the water
that wants to save you from drowning.
I know that certain things
may pass between two people
in the quiet hours,
words no longer necessary,
no longer spoken,
that bind them together,
two bodies of water
meeting for the first time, in the dark.

Uvalde

On the cell phone a child is crying
among the bodies of her dead
classmates,
unsure about how to ask for help.

The distance between
being shot
by a mad man with a high-powered assault rifle
at close range,
and the other side of the door

where police wait and do nothing,
is a million miles. Every day,
make them say their names.

The Names of Loss in English

My heart is a stone in your pocket
that you carry to remember
where you are.
Mercy should not be thought of
as a gift,
but as a natural genuflection
casting long shadows
across the lawns of the rich and the thoughtless.

My stone is a heart in your throat,
making it difficult
to swallow the truth,
the miles between us
barbed wire
strung across the sky.

I Went Mental

Pick a nightmare, pick a war, pick a single
sunlit shattered morning
and you may be allowed
entry into what looks
only like a maze from above
but that once you enter
becomes an endless cycle of trapdoors
where men and women gather in the dark,
not even far enough away
to let them talk out loud,
while the others, known as us,
camped nearby, but quiet for the night.
Some moments are impossible to let go of until you do.
Bullets make a sound going past your head
not like the sound of an insect, but something like that.
Voices are blurred by utter fear,
so it's impossible to understand
what anyone says.
Just then I leaped away, see? I checked out. I saw a door
open through the green place
and I walked through it.

For Bella, Dancing

I only knew you through the years from words
a sweet friend wrote to me
because she loved you and she wished you were hers,
and because she wanted me to love you too.
Once, she wrote and told me how you danced
so easily, on any occasion, and how
you'd lose yourself in your dance to make it come

alive. I don't like elegies, and the best
I can say about this world is that it's fucked
up when a child is allowed to die for no
reason but her mother and father's neglect. I want
to imagine that you're dancing, but that's only selfishness.
What's unjust stays unjust, no matter what,
and yet there is no standing still for you, even
as the shadows try to cling, and hold you down.
I know there is no standing still for you.

Notes on an English Novel

After many years
the man sees his lost wife
across the distance
and he describes her
in such a way
that we're given
rich details
about her character
and even about the nature
of her skin tone
in places we otherwise
would not be permitted to see, see?

Ghosts appear, briefly,
and ask for nothing.
It's the end of summer,
but no one moves on.

"If you feel me," someone says
at the picnic,
ruined by their desires,
and by the rain
that always never came.

When she returns,
after the dance,
she is different,
the house empty.

Whoever They Were

Whoever they were
swept into town
known as my house
like a clan of travelers
and settled in there
as if it was their own place.
They put their feet up
on the furniture
and complained about my cooking.
They argued with me
about my old opinions.
They stayed up late
then fell asleep with the lights and television on.
Carelessly, they let the dog out
then forgot about her
outside where she shivered in the cold.
They ate my food,
drank my whiskey,
smoked my cigarettes,
spent my money,
and used all my toilet paper.
Before they left they said they loved me,
and kissed me on the forehead, goodbye.
They kissed me on the forehead as they walked out the door.
They called me Papa, and said goodbye.

The Lake Will Take You Home

A man was crawling on Hàng Khay street
today. He moved slowly, in a combat

crawl along the sidewalk. No one helped him,
so I found a policeman, and in my sloppy Vietnamese,

I asked him why no one would help this man.
Điên cái đầu, he said in Vietnamese,

crazy, and he twirled his right index finger,
that universal sign. Soon, more police arrived,

and a crowd had gathered. The crawling man
stood up when a high-ranking officer

arrived and the man bowed to him as if
he was bowing to the Buddha, but the police captain

slapped his hands down and spoke roughly to him.
I could only understand a few words, but he was trying to tell

the man it was time to begin
walking home. The man stood only a few feet

from where I was, stupidly waiting to help.
He looked at me but our eyes wouldn't meet and he focused

his attention instead on the captain. He struggled to put his belt
back on, but when the captain saw the belt,

which had been torn in half and had no buckle,
he grabbed it and threw it in the nearby trash and the man

who'd been crawling, began to bow again,
holding his hands together in prayer. After another

hard smack across his back, he stopped ranting
and stood up straight. He was small, I saw for the first

time, and he thanked the policeman who walked
him across the busy street, dodging cars

the way they do here. On the other side
was the lake of the returned sword, Hồ Gươm,

the Vietnamese call it, that held an old
myth about finding the will to go on no matter

how complete the destruction of your life or your soul. People
walk around the lake day and night

until midnight. Mostly couples of all
ages, and some tourists. I watched him walk

to the edge of the lake before he began
to join with others around the perimeter, but no one

noticed him. He walked upright and held his head
high like he was headed to some worthy purpose. The police

captain was standing beside me, watching too.
He smiled at me and took his hat off. The crowd

had thinned. In Vietnamese he'd told the man to stand up, and walk home, around the lake.

The lake will take you home, he'd said.

Monk at Trấn Quốc

Go against the flow, the teacher says,
because there is no *flow*,

and no *against*,
another lesson I'd have to think about

for a long time and not be lazy
to understand. That's why we have

teachers, so tonight on Hồ Gươm,
the perfect lake in the center of the old city,

where people come all day and
most of the night to walk and watch the water,

and hold hands, perhaps
the only private moment they'll have all day.

Do you see? Can you feel the sudden
atmosphere of joy? It's nothing more than that.

The History of Blues in Hà Nội

The blues is the feeling
that you're not connected
to anything, or anyone,

and that *now*
is not a part of time.

End of winter,
the Đà trees
already trying to blossom.

Hồ Gươm Romance

The mist-covered lake
is like another world,
the ancient temple
only barely visible,

but ghost-like couples
still abide there,
holding their quiet hands
that they imagine
will keep them together.

Hàng Khay Night

I don't want to speak
to the rain again
but there's no escape
from these crowded
Hà Nội streets,
the shops and cafes
glazed with rain in such a sheen
I haven't seen before.

But it's what's inside the rain
I want to know,
what secret or magic
that could release us
from our suffering,
or else what good is it? And yet
the rain continues
to patter the new spring leaves,
a rhythm like a heartbeat, like
a heartbeat.

Our Fear of Hồ Gươm

The lake waits in the city,
as if it was lonely,
calling people to its shores. The lake
knows many secrets
it will not tell
about bodies
slipping in darkness
to the bottom
for centuries,
and bloody weapons
tossed
as if there was no end.

The lake doesn't like its name
and wants to change it
to the ancient word for water.
The lake breathes in and breathes out,
reminding us of its power.
The lake prays
at its own pagoda
then calls the mist
to settle in,
a curtain of lace,
a spring rain
released into the world
as if things
were going to be alright.

The lake says
things will not be alright,

not even close,
but the lake
shouldn't always
be believed,
things that
rise from the bottom,
like a sword
in the mouth
of a giant tortoise. How
convenient, how many lives.

Berserk

I tried to catch a quick *xê ôm*, a motorbike taxi,
all the way across the city, five o'clock,
the streets already clogged with traffic
coming, not going home. I was late for a meeting
that wouldn't wait
so I told him one hundred thousand
if he got me there on time,
and showed him on my watch.
Không sao, he said, no problem,
and I strapped on the too-small helmet
and climbed aboard. The first few
kilometers were fast,
zigzagging through traffic,
blowing red lights,
I was confident of my driver.
I enjoyed the ride.
But then traffic got thick and
our allotted time grew short
so he drove faster, sometimes
even driving on the sidewalk,
people walking there
startled into shouting as we passed.
When he pulled up
ahead of time,
I offered him a tip,
which he refused.

Now, Unattached to Time

Who is waiting in the empty hallway
that seems to know your name
the darkness asked itself.
What does the darkness want
except for more of the same,
like everyone else. Once
the law took the belt
and the swift hand
across the back,
away from parents,
everything changed,
and the power shifted. Later,
these same people
grew up with independent minds
and gathered in the streets
to try and stop an unjust war,
and they would raise children
who respected the earth.
It wasn't all bad, those days.
The war dragged on, that's true,
but more and more
people began to open their eyes,
especially when the loved ones
that they'd sent away
into what was called glory,
came back in black boxes
stacked up with the others
on a military runway, far
from where anyone could see.

Some Words for my Grandchildren

I wanted to tell you
that my old age
was your childhood,
and that none of us
knew what was next,
yet that was where the glory was,
the suddenness of knowing
you're inside a life
not entirely of your own choosing,
learning that the plentiful days
go by so quickly
it's hard to have anything at all.

I wanted to tell you that spirits
find refuge in the dark,
beside rivers hidden in the trees,
rivers who want to take you
down to their muddy bottoms,
all stones and dark debris,
askew in small tornadoes.
Don't go there, I want to tell you.
Let the lost have the night for themselves.

Marching with the Dead, on Bà Triệu

In a long procession down the street,
the mourners keep their heads down,
a flood of white circles passing, the procession
a way to see you off, proper,
come hell or high water,
and they have plenty of both here.

It must be someone important,
a friend says on the small balcony
overlooking the lake
where we say poems out loud and
drink too much homemade whiskey,
even for the night to bear.

It must be a poet,
someone else says
and everyone laughs.

What a peaceful place this is at ten p.m.,
lovers still walk the perimeter,
as in a ritual the body won't forget,
colored lights flick
on the surface,
a way you could go home on,
path of stars, path of graves of ancestors,
carry us home
before we no longer
remember the way back,
through whatever fucked up twilight
bullshit someone tries to throw over our heads like a net. Fuck that,

the starry sky said. Suck on this, said the moon,
and bite me,
said the night we put on, like a shirt.

A Brief Epistemology of Longing

The degrees of blue in the skies over Saigon
are heartbreaking in their intensity.

Where have all the old cars gone?
Where are all the birds?

And only sirens' sharp trill
fills night's windless avenues,

no birdsong. Only
lullaby of traffic noise, a different song.

How much you get back
depends upon how much you give,

plus or minus
a hundred years.

The Priority of Paradigms for Her

I was walking inside a life that was miserable, intolerable, empty.
Traffic sped past me fast, but I wasn't anywhere
in their plans on the roadway either. Sometimes
the sky will bend down
to scoop you up into the empty
is a secret someone told me once,
someone whispered into my ear and I believed,
all the way into the luxury
of what I could imagine.
Can you imagine?

You want to say that the sky
looks splintered into blue and white streaks,
islands in the stream.
You want to say a lot of things,
but a wall stands in the way.
What's green is already going to yellow,
and what departs
will always return
is a dream you may believe in
for how it gives shape
to everything else.
I *made* this poem for you, *làm thơ*.
I didn't write it. I know you understand.

In the Presence of Sympathetic Ghosts

To say a simple thing
even to the wind
that confesses its own emptiness. See
how quickly things can get out of control.
A man walks past, heat of afternoon,
wearing a woman's hat
decorated with a long feather
of unknown origin, but why not?
It's only time we have and
we only have it once. Sirens won't stop
etching into the long afternoon
but the man in the woman's hat
ignores them and crosses the busy street
as if it was empty. Don't wait any longer
for what you want, he seems to say,
it will come when it will.

I feel the earth revolve,
and that has to mean something,
that gravity is neither a good nor a bad thing,
the way rivers long only
to take us to their bottoms, the last surprise.
Oh sumptuous landscape,
allow me to drown in your flowers.
I promise to watch carefully where I step. I step
into the sky for once to find a way
from stone to burning stone
to arrive at the no answer, answer.
Be grateful for what you don't know, the da tree says
and looms above us

as we sleep the sleep of moon's
teeth in a wicked night,
of ghosts who don't belong
and only want to feed
on the loneliness. See
what streaks of white
crisscross the sky.

Dark Barges Churn the River White in the Moon

1
Phosphorescent particles of life
rise to city lights
held by the water's surface
just long enough for memory. Saigon
river, how did I find my way,
eighteen years old
plus nine months of jungle,
I couldn't believe my luck
to sleep in a dorm-like barrack
and have regular chow, three meals, every day.
I couldn't believe we were free,
to wander through the city as we pleased,
and the wild spirt I'd brought with me to war
took that invitation like a promise of everything
I couldn't allow to go unlived.

More than fifty years since that singular night,
nearly twenty thousand moons,
but what difference does time make
when the soul is at stake.
When the river is at stake,
what difference does the blue air make
to those swept away.

2
Whatever happened we have been made to remember,
over and over, modern
psychiatric medicine and therapy saw to that, line
up for your benefits as if a monthly dole could give you

back what was taken away, but in its place
a certain rawness came inside,
living on the torn edge of things
your only chance.

And whatever flowers were present are forgiven
their unrequited beauty. Only
truth will set you free, only
observing your actions
closely enough to see the cracks
and make your own sad song from what's left.

3

No value in the telling, I must show,
the words a wall of reeds
the light slides through like water,
the words as unreliable as a next breath.

I didn't understand what they wanted,
although I pretended that I did. Money
was involved,
and all I had to do was lead a fellow-
soldier to a room where a girl I didn't know
and had never seen, waited. Not knowing
is not a reason for forgiveness. I should have known.
I found a kid in the bar downstairs, already drunk, and
whispered into his ear and led him to that upstairs room.

Once he went inside,
but before they'd closed the door,
I saw through the opening
the naked body of a child on the bed. American

music playing on someone's radio.
I only had a glimpse
before they closed the door
but I spoke out anyway. I asked about her age.
I raised my voice in Vietnamese
and said it wasn't good,
and pointed to the now closed door.
The man in charge resisted, and soon,
two more men showed up and gently,
with strength I could feel as they held me,
led me away down the stairs.

Out on the street the man handed me the money.
I didn't need it, or want it, but I took it anyway.

4

Some days come easy as blossoms in spring,
their slow indulgence of the world
a lesson in how to live. Some days
haunt like a shroud you can't throw off,
and your only chance is to choose a path
through the dark trees of memory
and hope for an escape. Isn't that all we want,
and doesn't the wheel that time is
return with the same impossible
spinning of what was taken away and what was given back.

5

The return of inevitable stars
provides comfort to an aching body, even this late.
Stylish night overtakes us
until the poorer quarters

are blurred at the edges,
and impossible to see any longer. Jazz music

seeps from the open window
of an upstairs club on the river,
the silent barges
slipping past like all of memory.
A saxophone blows Coltrane, sweet,
More lasting than bronze,
the notes like words that say,
I am what you were,
and now you are known.

Meditation at Bao Vinh, Among Roses

I
Whatever happens,
the shadow of the woman's
head begins at her feet.

II
The end is near.
Two red and brown
wrens flit on the balcony.

III
The solitary woman
ignites the air,
cold as a broken promise.

Temporal Reality Take Out for A.

When they talk about equivalence, relevance, his elegance
        I'm not certain that bells ring against
                what wants to take the avalanche

like a chance to resist look
        how we can persist when our hearts are in it
                it looked like a mist to begin with

the tale of small red flowers
        in the wind not a waste of hours or a sin,
                but a din and nothing to do with the fall

of anything important at all, not a knock down drag out
        you're resorting to but they got their flags out
                just like in boarding school. No it's not the same,

it's not the rhyme that matters, but it's the chatter to blame.
        It's not the mind that's in tatters, rather a vein
                opened up, mad hatter came and gone through the pain.

I heard his footsteps patter across the floor
        and this is all before the rendezvous
                for every after there has to be a before, so where are you

for every disaster you hope for even more
        of the same and what's to blame for that
                but broken landscapes and how we adapt

say your name I want to say your name to open that gate
the broken tree limbs scattered after the storm are only
that and not my fate or yours. Blue sky bring us home
again, one more time,

so we can live inside the dome that's been our home beyond
the bind the world will sometimes put you in no matter how
your mind wants to choose what the blues mean for yourself,
the sign that you use

if you're found in the rain, without shoes, say.
I had tried to teach you what had saved me more than once:
you run towards the fire, and not away.

What Nhung Wrote Down

A poem about being
safe inside of poetry
in her notebook
when she
lived at the factory
where she worked
for two years
saving her wages
to attend the Nguyễn Du
writing school in Hà Nội
where her talent
blossomed like a Đà tree
in spring. You must have
the skills, she said,
to hide your emotions,
Fleetwood Mac
on the radio,
a song about
the sound doves make, that
oh, oh, oh
they send out,
an invitation
of the most intimate kind.

Red Bridge on Hoàn Kiếm Lake

Soul of the witch with all ten fingers,
soul of the brooch she used to tie back her hair.
She'd lost her ability to propositionize,
to say a single word.

If god is free to take, god is not free,
or so the story goes.
The sky had not yet untied the day
but there was always the weight of sadness,

the bright yellow star on the huge red flag
that furls and unfurls in the breeze

Night Message, From a Friend

I was cold
because I had carried the warmth of your life in my body. You left me here.

But the sky was not so vast I had to close my eyes,
and the defeat not so accurate

so as to leave me with nothing.
The night's scarred face is something.

Going Back

You can say
What's the fucking point,
the river of heaven turns in the night
no matter what history you rely upon,
like your own, for example,

or what moments you return to,
a blind rat to its hole in the house
occupied by something
disturbed yet not quite hidden
in the walls is how I remember it,

and how do you explain those forces
to your friends?
Through the darkest rooms
you follow the brightest light,
no matter what.

An Ars Poetica

in memory of my teacher, Charlie Simic

Although the answer isn't always rain,
I come to that again, the sound
like pity through the empty trees, a vast
gray sky that opens to the coming dark.
What is this longing to know
even the pain that must abide in us all,
and to see into things deep enough
to feel, I don't know, but only the emptiness
lasts forever, and the rain continues
to fall like vaguely made promises
through the not yet frozen branches. See,
not everything means something in that ordinary way,
and what's measured and accounted for
is often lost before we even see its brilliance.
This is the nature of poetry and death,
how every end of line is like
a precipice you must discover
in the dark to make your way,
the last distinguished thing.

Notes

In "*Mưa Xuân*," the title means "spring rain," a fine, mist-like rain that comes frequently during the spring in the north, and is most often ignored by everyone, who go about their business nevertheless.

In the poem "Loving the Jungle Blues," I borrow from the song "Wish You Were Here," by Pink Floyd.

The title "Tôi đi bộ quanh hồ Hà Lê" means "I walk around Hà Lê Lake," a small lake on Nguyễn Du Street in Hà Nội.

"The Names of Loss in English," is inspired by David Young's poem, "The Names of the Hare in English."

In the poem "Hàng Khay Night," the street, Hàng Khay, is one that borders Hồ Gươm, the central lake in the city of Hà Nội, and the source of the returned sword myth.

"Night Message, From a Friend," is based on lines from Dulce Maria Laynaz, from the collection *Absolute Solitude: Selected Poems.*

"Marching with the Dead, on Bà Triệu" alludes to the public funeral processions that are common in Việt Nam and to which strangers are invited to join all along the way.

The last stanza of "Dark Barges Churn the River White in the Moon," is based on lines from Cipriano de Valera.

The poem, "Temporal Reality Take Out for A.," is inspired by rap lyrics by Andrew Kondo Weigl.

Acknowledgments

I offer my grateful acknowledgment for the support of editors of magazines in which these poems first appeared.

Consequence: "Marching with the Dead, on Bà Triệu";

Eunoia Review: "Autumn, End of Everything," and "The Dangers of Searching the Photographs of Reynaldo Sandoval";

Innisfree: "The Dangers of Searching the Photographs of Reynaldo Sandoval," "Being and Listening," "Saying Goodbye to Achill," "Dark Barges Churn the River White in the Moon," "Night Message, From a Friend";

Pulse and Echo: "The Weight of Rain," "The Ambiguity of His Intentions," "The Apostle of Desire," "Lost Episode," "Homage to the Gecko";

Rattle: "Thinking About Her," "Outside Quảng Trị City, 1968";

TriQuarterly: "The Lake Will Take You Home";

War, Literature, and the Arts: "Outside Quảng Trị City, 1968," "A Simple Lesson," "Why I Love my Doctor," "My Bill Evans."

Many of these poems were written during several long residencies in Việt Nam. I am especially grateful to Nguyễn Quang Thiều, President of the Việt Nam Writers Association, for his support and for the support of his excellent staff at Hội Nhà Văn, in Hà Nội. I am grateful also to the writing community of Hà Nội for welcoming me among them. Without this support, I would not have been able to freely do my work as a translator and poet, wherever I might find myself working. My thanks go to my Vietnamese friends for teaching me the difference between "going home," and "coming home."

In the south, in Hồ Chí Minh City, where I spent a month working mostly in solitude on this manuscript, I had the generous support of my friend, the poet Trần Lê Khánh, and his kind family. This time of self-imposed isolation, away from the telephone and other distractions, and well taken care of by Khánh's staff, in a beautifully comfortable space, allowed me time to complete work on this manuscript. I remain grateful for their support and for their enduring friendship.

I am also grateful for the help, support, and friendship of the writer, blogger, translator and interpreter, Mai Trang, whose invaluable contributions in Hà Nội helped make my work possible.

Finally, I am also grateful to Peter Conners for his enduring support of my work, and for his devoted and talented staff at BOA, to Reginald Gibbons for his friendship and the gift of his poems, and to David Keplinger, who helped me put the final version of this manuscript together. Thanks also to Peter Nguyễn for his assistance with the Vietnamese diacritics throughout this manuscript, and as always, I am grateful to my wife Jean Kondo, for her long support of my writing life.

Dedications

"*Mưa Xuân*" is for Nhuệ Anh.

"Verse Thirteen" is for Trần Lê Khánh.

"The First Time I Heard Your Name, it was Different" is for my daughter, Nguyễn Thị Hạnh Willbond.

"The Dangers of Searching the Photographs of Reynaldo Sandoval" is for my friend, RS.

"Epistolary to a Brother" is for SL.

"The New Road Neighborhood Showdown" is for Mayor David Leshinski.

"Why I Flunked Philosophy 301" is in memory of David Love.

"Saying Goodbye to Achill" is for John Deane.

"The History of Blues in Hà Nội" is for Mai Trang.

About the Author

Born in Lorain, Ohio in 1949, Bruce Weigl is the author of fourteen books of verse including *The Abundance of Nothing* (2012), a finalist for the Pulitzer Prize in Poetry, and *Song of Napalm* (1988), a Pulitzer Prize nominee. In 2019, BOA Editions, Ltd. published *On the Shores of Welcome Home,* winner of the Isabella Gardner Poetry Award, as well as his prose poems, *Among Elms, in Ambush,* in 2021. Weigl served in Vietnam from 1967-1968, where he earned The Bronze Star, returning home to study poetry at Oberlin College. Since 1988, he has regularly returned to Hà Nội, working with the Vietnamese Writers Association, whose members have translated several of his poems; in turn Weigl has translated the poetry of Vietnamese soldiers *(Poems from Captured Documents)* and the masterpiece of Tran Le Khanh, *The Sum of Now: the One Thousand Poems.* Weigl's celebrated memoir of the war and his return to Vietnam is *The Circle of Hanh* (2000). His work has garnered many honors, including the Robert Creeley Award, the Paterson Poetry Prize, and the Poet's Prize from the Academy of American Poets. For his artistic contributions and poetic vision, Bruce Weigl received the Lannan Literary Award in 2006 as well as awards for his "distinguished contributions to the translation and teaching of Vietnamese poetry," from *Hoi Nha Van*, the Vietnamese Writers Association.

BOA Editions, Ltd. American Poets Continuum Series

No. 1 *The Fuhrer Bunker: A Cycle of Poems in Progress*
W. D. Snodgrass

No. 2 *She*
M. L. Rosenthal

No. 3 *Living With Distance*
Ralph J. Mills, Jr.

No. 4 *Not Just Any Death*
Michael Waters

No. 5 *That Was Then: New and Selected Poems*
Isabella Gardner

No. 6 *Things That Happen Where There Aren't Any People*
William Stafford

No. 7 *The Bridge of Change: Poems 1974–1980*
John Logan

No. 8 *Signatures*
Joseph Stroud

No. 9 *People Live Here: Selected Poems 1949–1983*
Louis Simpson

No. 10 *Yin*
Carolyn Kizer

No. 11 *Duhamel: Ideas of Order in Little Canada*
Bill Tremblay

No. 12 *Seeing It Was So*
Anthony Piccione

No. 13 *Hyam Plutzik: The Collected Poems*

No. 14 *Good Woman: Poems and a Memoir 1969–1980*
Lucille Clifton

No. 15 *Next: New Poems*
Lucille Clifton

No. 16 *Roxa: Voices of the Culver Family*
William B. Patrick

No. 17 *John Logan: The Collected Poems*

No. 18 *Isabella Gardner: The Collected Poems*

No. 19 *The Sunken Lightship*
Peter Makuck

No. 20 *The City in Which I Love You*
Li-Young Lee

No. 21 *Quilting: Poems 1987–1990*
Lucille Clifton

No. 22 *John Logan: The Collected Fiction*

No. 23 *Shenandoah and Other Verse Plays*
Delmore Schwartz

No. 24 *Nobody Lives on Arthur Godfrey Boulevard*
Gerald Costanzo

No. 25 *The Book of Names: New and Selected Poems*
Barton Sutter

No. 26 *Each in His Season*
W. D. Snodgrass

No. 27 *Wordworks: Poems Selected and New*
Richard Kostelanetz

No. 28 *What We Carry*
Dorianne Laux

No. 29 *Red Suitcase*
Naomi Shihab Nye

No. 30 *Song*
Brigit Pegeen Kelly

No. 31 *The Fuehrer Bunker: The Complete Cycle*
W. D. Snodgrass

No. 32 *For the Kingdom*
Anthony Piccione

No. 33 *The Quicken Tree*
Bill Knott

No. 34 *These Upraised Hands*
William B. Patrick

No. 35 *Crazy Horse in Stillness*
William Heyen

No. 36 *Quick, Now, Always*
Mark Irwin

No. 37 *I Have Tasted the Apple*
Mary Crow

No. 38 *The Terrible Stories*
Lucille Clifton

No. 39 *The Heat of Arrivals*
Ray Gonzalez

No. 40 *Jimmy & Rita*
Kim Addonizio

No. 41 *Green Ash, Red Maple, Black Gum*
Michael Waters

No. 42 *Against Distance*
Peter Makuck

No. 43 *The Night Path*
Laurie Kutchins

No. 44 *Radiography*
Bruce Bond

No. 45 *At My Ease: Uncollected Poems of the Fifties and Sixties*
David Ignatow

No. 46 *Trillium*
Richard Foerster

No. 47 *Fuel*
Naomi Shihab Nye

No. 48 *Gratitude*
Sam Hamill

No. 49 *Diana, Charles, & the Queen*
William Heyen

No. 50 *Plus Shipping*
Bob Hicok

No. 51 *Cabato Sentora*
Ray Gonzalez

No. 52 *We Didn't Come Here for This*
William B. Patrick

No. 53 *The Vandals*
Alan Michael Parker

No. 54 *To Get Here*
Wendy Mnookin

No. 55 *Living Is What I Wanted: Last Poems*
David Ignatow

No. 56 *Dusty Angel*
Michael Blumenthal

No. 57 *The Tiger Iris*
Joan Swift

No. 58 *White City*
Mark Irwin

No. 59 *Laugh at the End of the World: Collected Comic Poems 1969–1999*
Bill Knott

No. 60 *Blessing the Boats: New and Selected Poems: 1988–2000*
Lucille Clifton

No. 61 *Tell Me*
Kim Addonizio

No. 62 *Smoke*
Dorianne Laux

No. 63 *Parthenopi: New and Selected Poems*
Michael Waters

No. 64 *Rancho Notorious*
Richard Garcia

No. 65 *Jam*
Joe-Anne McLaughlin

No. 66 *A. Poulin, Jr. Selected Poems*
Edited, with an Introduction by Michael Waters

No. 67 *Small Gods of Grief*
Laure-Anne Bosselaar

No. 68 *Book of My Nights*
Li-Young Lee

No. 69 *Tulip Farms and Leper Colonies*
Charles Harper Webb

No. 70 *Double Going*
Richard Foerster

No. 71 *What He Took*
Wendy Mnookin

No. 72 *The Hawk Temple at Tierra Grande*
Ray Gonzalez

No. 73 *Mules of Love*
Ellen Bass

No. 74 *The Guests at the Gate*
Anthony Piccione

No. 75 *Dumb Luck*
Sam Hamill

No. 76 *Love Song with Motor Vehicles*
Alan Michael Parker

No. 77 *Life Watch*
Willis Barnstone

No. 78 *The Owner of the House: New Collected Poems 1940–2001*
Louis Simpson

No. 79 *Is*
Wayne Dodd

No. 80 *Late*
Cecilia Woloch

No. 81 *Precipitates*
Debra Kang Dean

No. 82 *The Orchard*
Brigit Pegeen Kelly

No. 83 *Bright Hunger*
Mark Irwin

No. 84 *Desire Lines: New and Selected Poems*
Lola Haskins

No. 85 *Curious Conduct*
Jeanne Marie Beaumont

No. 86 *Mercy*
Lucille Clifton

No. 87 *Model Homes*
Wayne Koestenbaum

No. 88 *Farewell to the Starlight in Whiskey*
Barton Sutter

No. 89 *Angels for the Burning*
David Mura

No. 90 *The Rooster's Wife*
Russell Edson

No. 91 *American Children*
Jim Simmerman

No. 92 *Postcards from the Interior*
Wyn Cooper

No. 93 *You & Yours*
Naomi Shihab Nye

No. 94 *Consideration of the Guitar: New and Selected Poems 1986–2005*
Ray Gonzalez

No. 95 *Off-Season in the Promised Land*
Peter Makuck

No. 96 *The Hoopoe's Crown*
Jacqueline Osherow

No. 97 *Not for Specialists: New and Selected Poems*
W. D. Snodgrass

No. 98 *Splendor*
Steve Kronen

No. 99 *Woman Crossing a Field*
Deena Linett

No. 100 *The Burning of Troy*
Richard Foerster

No. 101 *Darling Vulgarity*
Michael Waters

No. 102 *The Persistence of Objects*
Richard Garcia

No. 103 *Slope of the Child Everlasting*
Laurie Kutchins

No. 104 *Broken Hallelujahs*
Sean Thomas Dougherty

No. 105 *Peeping Tom's Cabin: Comic Verse 1928–2008*
X. J. Kennedy

No. 106 *Disclamor*
G.C. Waldrep

No. 107 *Encouragement for a Man Falling to His Death*
Christopher Kennedy

No. 108 *Sleeping with Houdini*
Nin Andrews

No. 109 *Nomina*
Karen Volkman

No. 110 *The Fortieth Day*
Kazim Ali

No. 111 *Elephants & Butterflies*
Alan Michael Parker

No. 112 *Voices*
Lucille Clifton

No. 113 *The Moon Makes Its Own Plea*
Wendy Mnookin

No. 114 *The Heaven-Sent Leaf*
Katy Lederer

No. 115 *Struggling Times*
Louis Simpson

No. 116 *And*
Michael Blumenthal

No. 117 *Carpathia*
Cecilia Woloch

No. 118 *Seasons of Lotus, Seasons of Bone*
Matthew Shenoda

No. 119 *Sharp Stars*
Sharon Bryan

No. 120 *Cool Auditor*
Ray Gonzalez

No. 121 *Long Lens: New and Selected Poems*
Peter Makuck

No. 122 *Chaos Is the New Calm*
Wyn Cooper

No. 123 *Diwata*
Barbara Jane Reyes

No. 124 *Burning of the Three Fires*
Jeanne Marie Beaumont

No. 125 *Sasha Sings the Laundry on the Line*
Sean Thomas Dougherty

No. 126 *Your Father on the Train of Ghosts*
G.C. Waldrep and John Gallaher

No. 127 *Ennui Prophet*
Christopher Kennedy

No. 128 *Transfer*
Naomi Shihab Nye

No. 129 *Gospel Night*
Michael Waters

No. 130 *The Hands of Strangers: Poems from the Nursing Home*
Janice N. Harrington

No. 131 *Kingdom Animalia*
Aracelis Girmay

No. 132 *True Faith*
Ira Sadoff

No. 133 *The Reindeer Camps and Other Poems*
Barton Sutter

No. 134 *The Collected Poems of Lucille Clifton: 1965–2010*

No. 135 *To Keep Love Blurry*
Craig Morgan Teicher

No. 136 *Theophobia*
Bruce Beasley

No. 137 *Refuge*
Adrie Kusserow

No. 138 *The Book of Goodbyes*
Jillian Weise

No. 139 *Birth Marks*
Jim Daniels

No. 140 *No Need of Sympathy*
Fleda Brown

No. 141 *There's a Box in the Garage You Can Beat with a Stick*
Michael Teig

No. 142 *The Keys to the Jail*
Keetje Kuipers

No. 143 *All You Ask for Is Longing: New and Selected Poems 1994–2014*
Sean Thomas Dougherty

No. 144 *Copia*
Erika Meitner

No. 145 *The Chair: Prose Poems*
Richard Garcia

No. 146 *In a Landscape*
John Gallaher

No. 147 *Fanny Says*
Nickole Brown

No. 148 *Why God Is a Woman*
Nin Andrews

No. 149 *Testament*
G.C. Waldrep

No. 150 *I'm No Longer Troubled by the Extravagance*
Rick Bursky

No. 151 *Antidote for Night*
Marsha de la O

No. 152 *Beautiful Wall*
Ray Gonzalez

No. 153 *the black maria*
Aracelis Girmay

No. 154 *Celestial Joyride*
Michael Waters

No. 155 *Whereso*
Karen Volkman

No. 156 *The Day's Last Light Reddens the Leaves of the Copper Beech*
Stephen Dobyns

No. 157 *The End of Pink*
Kathryn Nuernberger

No. 158 *Mandatory Evacuation*
Peter Makuck

No. 159 *Primitive: The Art and Life of Horace H. Pippin*
Janice N. Harrington

No. 160 *The Trembling Answers*
Craig Morgan Teicher

No. 161 *Bye-Bye Land*
Christian Barter

No. 162 *Sky Country*
Christine Kitano

No. 163 *All Soul Parts Returned*
Bruce Beasley

No. 164 *The Smoke of Horses*
Charles Rafferty

No. 165 *The Second O of Sorrow*
Sean Thomas Dougherty

No. 166 *Holy Moly Carry Me*
Erika Meitner

No. 167 *Clues from the Animal Kingdom*
Christopher Kennedy

No. 168 *Dresses from the Old Country*
Laura Read

No. 169 *In Country*
Hugh Martin

No. 170 *The Tiny Journalist*
Naomi Shihab Nye

No. 171 *All Its Charms*
Keetje Kuipers

No. 172 *Night Angler*
Geffrey Davis

No. 173 *The Human Half*
Deborah Brown

No. 174 *Cyborg Detective*
Jillian Weise

No. 175 *On the Shores of Welcome Home*
Bruce Weigl

No. 176 *Rue*
Kathryn Nuernberger

No. 177 *Let's Become a Ghost Story*
Rick Bursky

No. 178 *Year of the Dog*
Deborah Paredez

No. 179 *Brand New Spacesuit*
John Gallaher

No. 180 *How to Carry Water: Selected Poems of Lucille Clifton*
Edited, with an Introduction by Aracelis Girmay

No. 181 *Caw*
Michael Waters

No. 182 *Letters to a Young Brown Girl*
Barbara Jane Reyes

No. 183 *Mother Country*
Elana Bell

No. 184 *Welcome to Sonnetville, New Jersey*
Craig Morgan Teicher

No. 185 *I Am Not Trying to Hide My Hungers from the World*
Kendra DeColo

No. 186 *The Naomi Letters*
Rachel Mennies

No. 187 *Tenderness*
Derrick Austin

No. 188 *Ceive*
B.K. Fischer

No. 189 *Diamonds*
Camille Guthrie

No. 190 *A Cluster of Noisy Planets*
Charles Rafferty

No. 191 *Useful Junk*
Erika Meitner

No. 192 *Field Notes from the Flood Zone*
Heather Sellers

No. 193 *A Season in Hell with Rimbaud*
Dustin Pearson

No. 194 *Your Emergency Contact Has Experienced an Emergency*
Chen Chen

No. 195 *A Tinderbox in Three Acts*
Cynthia Dewi Oka

No. 196 *Little Mr. Prose Poem: Selected Poems of Russell Edson*
Edited by Craig Morgan Teicher

No. 197 *The Dug-Up Gun Museum*
Matt Donovan

No. 198 *Four in Hand*
Alicia Mountain

No. 199 *Buffalo Girl*
Jessica Q. Stark

No. 200 *Nomenclatures of Invisibility*
Mahtem Shiferraw

No. 201 *Flare, Corona*
Jeannine Hall Gailey

No. 202 *Death Prefers the Minor Keys*
Sean Thomas Dougherty

No. 203 *Desire Museum*
Danielle Deulen

No. 204 *Transitory*
Subhaga Crystal Bacon

No. 205 *Every Hard Sweetness*
Sheila Carter-Jones

No. 206 *Blue on a Blue Palette*
Lynne Thompson

No. 207 *One Wild Word Away*
Geffrey Davis

No. 208 *The Strange God Who Makes Us*
Christopher Kennedy

No. 209 *Our Splendid Failure to Do the Impossible*
Rebecca Lindenberg

No. 210 *Yard Show*
Janice N. Harrington

No. 211 *The Last Song of the World*
Joseph Fasano

No. 212 *Lonely Women Make Good Lovers*
Keetje Kuipers

No. 213 *jump the gun*
Jennie Malboeuf

No. 214 *Apostle of Desire*
Bruce Weigl

Colophon

BOA Editions, Ltd., a not-for-profit publisher of poetry and other literary works, fosters readership and appreciation of contemporary literature. By identifying, cultivating, and publishing both new and established poets and selecting authors of unique literary talent, BOA brings high-quality literature to the public.

Support for this effort comes from the sale of its publications, grant funding, and private donations.

*

The publication of this book is made possible, in part, by the special support of the following individuals:

Anonymous
Angela Bonazinga & Catherine Lewis
Ralph Black & Susan Murphy
Chris Dahl, *in honor of Chuck Hertrick*
Jonathan Everitt
David Fraher, *in memory of A. Poulin Jr.*
Bonnie Garner
James Hale
Peg Heminway
Grant Holcomb
Nora A. Jones
Joe & Dale Klein
Barbara Lovenheim, *in memory of John Lovenheim*
Hugh Martin & Sarah Mullens,
in memory of SPC. Nicholaus Zimmer
Joe McElveney
Daniel M. Meyers, *in honor of J. Shepard Skiff*
Boo Poulin, *in memory of A. Poulin Jr.*
Deborah Ronnen
John H. Schultz
William Waddell & Linda Rubel
Michael Waters & Mihaela Moscaliuc